William Henry Whitmore

The cavalier

An essay on the origin of the founders of the thirteen colonies

William Henry Whitmore

The cavalier
An essay on the origin of the founders of the thirteen colonies

ISBN/EAN: 9783337153410

Printed in Europe, USA, Canada, Australia, Japan

Cover: Foto ©ninafisch / pixelio.de

More available books at **www.hansebooks.com**

THE CAVALIER DISMOUNTED:

AN ESSAY

ON THE ORIGIN OF THE FOUNDERS OF THE

THIRTEEN COLONIES.

" We are the gentlemen of this country."

ROBERT TOOMBS, in 1860.

" Our Plantations in America, *New England excepted*, have been generally settled, 1, by Malcontents with the Administrations from Time to Time; 2. by fraudulent Debtors, as a refuge from their Creditors; and by Convicts or Criminals, who chose Transportation rather than Death."

Dr. WILLIAM DOUGLASS, 1749.

BY

WILLIAM H. WHITMORE,

MEMBER OF THE MASSACHUSETTS HISTORICAL SOCIETY, AND OF THE
NEW-ENGLAND HISTORIC-GENEALOGICAL SOCIETY.

SALEM:
PUBLISHED BY G. M. WHIPPLE & A. A. SMITH.

1864.

PREFACE.

This essay is an enlargement of an article which appeared in the Continental Magazine for June, 1863. The additions are mainly of authorities quoted, and though but a portion of the writer's collections are here printed, it is presumed that there are enough to substantiate his assertions. Two points are intended to be discussed. The first is the proportion of native-born citizens in the United States, descended from the inhabitants in 1790. The second is the origin of the ancestors of the colonists.

The result of investigations of the first point, differs widely from the opinion of recent journalists. In the New York Shipping-List for Sept. 24th, 1864, will be found a statement, that the natural increase of the colonists of 1790, would amount to only eight millions out of nearly thirty millions, now inhabiting the United States. If there be no mistake in the table prepared from the official Census of the United States, the reverse of this statement is the truth. Twenty millions of our citizens were in 1860 descended from our original colonists, and only six and one half millions were foreign-born or descended from immigrants arriving here since 1790.

This question is one of too great importance to remain thus doubtful. Our nationality is a stubborn fact ; and the question is to be solved whether we are formed from a heterogenous collection of all nationalities, or have in reality one predominant race which gives its tone to the whole. The opinion herein expressed is, that the English race predominates here, and that the reason of its influence is to be found in the fact that New England was so intensely English. If the figures be correct, New England has contributed one quarter or one third of the population of the country, and this portion has constantly allied itself to the English part of the remainder of our population. Hence the preponderance of the English language, laws and national characteristics.

As to the second point, our investigations have been mainly directed toward the correction of false statements made by the Rebel emissaries and press. It is not a grateful task to be obliged to ex-

This matter of purity of race is one of no trivial importance. It would be contrary to the spirit of our institutions for us to attempt to give to ancestral claims the importance which attach to them in monarchical countries; and yet this very rebellion teaches us that there are important problems connected with the subject which even republicans cannot ignore.

We have seen in one portion of our Union, a dominant class, small in number, but allied in interest, successfully leading astray multitudes whose true interests were diametrically opposed to any revolt; and we have seen in the other portion, vast communities holding firm allegiance to written laws, yielding unswerving obedience to their duly appointed authorities, and, despite apparent diversities of origin and interests, maintaining themselves in the bonds of an imperishable union.

The Southerners and their English allies have claimed that their unanimity proceeded from their common origin and gentle parentage; the unanimity of the North they have long denied and can now regard only as inexplicable. We hold on the contrary that the North is united because that it is homogeneous, and that the apparent unanimity of the South is only enforced by a vigorous tyranny, founded upon centuries of oppression and possible only through the faulty construction of its early institutions.

That there has been a wide diversity in the construction of society, North and South, from the commencement of the colonies of Virginia and New England, is undisputable. Accident has brought these original peculiarities in antagonism, but we must not be misled as to their true significance.

In the Southern Colonies, as will be proved, society received a form somewhat analogous to that of the England of two centuries ago; an aristocratic form, a base and spurious imitation of a bad original, was imposed upon the infant settlements. In England in 1630, the rank of the gentry was established, and it had a certain meaning and cause. This modified form of feudalism had a reasonable foundation. The great land-owners were a distinct class from their tenants aud inferiors; they were the natural leaders and rulers according to the rule of progression which had elevated the entire community from the barbarism of the feudal ages. The country gentleman, whose family had been known and respected for four centuries, seemed a natural chief to those whose ancestors had during that period owned allegiance to the name. To this class had been confined nearly all of the wealth, valor and culture of the nation.

When Virginia and the other Southern Atlantic colonies were planted, however, the emigrants took with them but the empty form of their native customs. As will be proved, very few of them possessed any hereditary claim to the rank of gentlemen, and even these were without the indispensible body of hereditary retainers, in whom a reverential submission was a matter of faith.

In a country where a man's daily food depended upon his daily labor, where patents of land embraced leagues, and where equality was a necessity, what chance was there even for the best blood of England to establish an aristocracy?

In the true sense, in the signification yet attached to the word in Europe, they never did establish an aristocracy, yet they founded an imitation which has yearly become more despicable. Instead of tenants, the new aristocrats peopled their lands with black slaves, or white convicts bound to them for a term of years. As a natural consequence their aristocracy became composed not of those who had hereditary rank,—not of gentry in the English sense,—but of all those who could invest capital in flesh and blood. In Virginia and the Carolinas, the slave-owners usurped the name of gentlemen; they had a sufficient intermixture of that class to serve as a screen, and there were none to question their claims.

Yet it must be borne in mind that these absurd claims have been pushed offensively only within the last few years. We have yet to learn that during colonial times or the dark period of the Revolution, any superiority was claimed by the South over the North. It has only been since our national prosperity became so great, that these false aspersions have been indulged in, and a Cavalier has presumed to arrogate a precedence over a Puritan.

To prove the inherent absurdity of the claims of the South, I beg leave to present certain tables compiled from the official Census returns.

I assume in the following table that the inhabitants of the United States in 1790 were citizens by birth, and by deducting at the end of each decade the number of immigrants, we have what may fairly be claimed as the percentage of natural increase. I have added the slight excess over the percentage to the column of native born, believing this advantage at least belongs to them:

WHITE POPULATION OF THE UNITED STATES.

TABLE No. 1.—INCREASE AND IMMIGRATION.

Date.	Pr ct. of natural increase	Total per Census.	Natives. 1790	Aliens. 1800	Aliens. 1810	Aliens. 1820	Aliens. 1830	Aliens. 1840	Aliens. 1850	Aliens. 1860
1790	33.7	3,172,464	3,172,464 1,071,971	50,000						
1800	34.4	4,294,435	4,244,435 1,465,290	50,000 16,200	70,000					
1810	32.1	5,845,925	5,700,725 1,835,672	66,200 21,250	70,000 22,470	114.000				
1820	32.1	7,839,317	7,545,397 2,424,228	87,450 28,071	92,470 29,781	114,000 36,594	151,824			
1830	29	10,509,815	9,909,625 2,899,444	115,521 33,501	122.251 35,452	150.594 43,673	161,824 44,028	509,125		
1840	25.1	14,165,038	12,869,069 3,238,699	149,022 37,448	157,703 39,583	194,267 48,761	195,852 49,157	509,125 150,380	1,713,251	
1850	23.9	19,442,272	16,107,768 3,868,994	186,425 44,456	197,296 47,151	243,028 58,083	245,009 58,557	749,505 179,131	1,713,251 409,467	2,598,214
1860		26,706,425	19,976,762	230,881	244,437	301,111	303,566	928,636	2,122,718	2,598,214

This table shows us that in the States in 1860, out of 26,706,425 white inhabitants, 19,976,762 were the descendants of the original citizens of 1790. I omit the territories, as the number of inhabitants cannot affect the result, and it is difficult to decide upon their nationality.

In Table II, I propose to divide the inhabitants of 1790 into four classes, the first comprising New England; the second, New York, New Jersey, and Pennsylvania; the third, Virginia, North Carolina, South Carolina, and Georgia; and the fourth, Delaware, Maryland, Kentucky and Tennessee.

Allowing to each class the same percentage of increase as in the former table, we shall see how our nineteen millions of native-born citizens originated:

Date.	Per cent. of Increase.	Total as per "Native" column, Table No. 1.	New England.	New York &c.	Virginia &c.	Delaware &c.
1790	33.7	3,172,464	992,781 335,417	908,195 306,911	923,383 312,030	348,105 117,613
1800	34.4	4,244,435	1,328,198 458,465	1,215,106 419,596	1,235,413 426,582	465,718 160,647
1810	32.1	5,709,725	1,786,663 574,369	1,634,702 525,589	1,661,995 534,350	626,365 201,364
1820	32.1	7,545,397	2,361,032 758,541	2,160,291 694,103	2,196,345 705,676	827,729 265,908
1830	29	9,969,625	3,119,573 907,176	2,854,394 830,274	2,902,021 844,086	1,093,637 317,908
1840	25.1	12,869,069	4,026,749 1,012,464	3,684,668 927,852	3,746,107 943,272	1,411,545 355,111
1850	23.9	16,107,768	5,039,213 1,210,270	4,612,520 1,108,292	4,689,379 1,126,661	1,766,656 423,771
1860		19,976,762	6,249,483	5,720,812	5,816,040	2,190,427

Here then we see that New England has contributed nearly one third of the number, and nearly one quarter of the entire population.

But I will endeavor further to analyze the constitution of the different States which were added to the Union previous to 1860. The following table will show the numbers at each decade:

Date.	FREE STATES.			SLAVE STATES.		
	Inhabitants per Census.	Natives.	Immigrants.	Inhabitants all Native.	Immigrants.	Immigrants.
1810	3,653,219	3,421,365	231,854	2,192,706	95,654	
1820	5,030,371	4,521,323	509,048	2,808,946	215,048	
1830	6,874,302	5,973,967	900,335	3,635,513	360,145	
1840	9,560,165	7,711,417	1,848,748	4,604,873	552,779	
1850	13,257,795	9,651,733	3,606,062	6,184,477	271,558	
1860	17,993,585	11,970,295	6,023,290	8,712,840	....	706,373

We have now certain data from which to argue, and I will first investigate the alleged homogeneity of the South. Conceding that every citizen of the two classes of Virginia, etc., and Delaware, etc., in 1790, was indisputably the descendant of an English cavalier, and that the increase of population found an outlet into the new Slave States, how would the case stand?

In 1860 these states contained 8,712,840; by Table II we calculated they should contain 8,006,467; so that even in this case there are some 700,000 foreigners. But a little more research shows that the case is much more unfavorble.

Up to 1840, the Southern States not only could have furnished all the settlers in the Slave States, but must have sent out colonists. In 1840, they had 4,604,873 inhabitants; add to this the natural increase, 25.1 per cent, (1,155,823,) and we have 5,760,696 native born, and 423,781 foreigners required to make their total of 6,184,477 inhabitants.

But in the next decade, add to the 5,760,696 native born their percentage of increase, 23.9 (1,376,806,) and we have 7,137,502, requiring 1,575,338 foreigners, *more than one sixth*, for their total of 8,712,840 white inhabitants.

By no conceivable chance can more than five sixths of the population of the South be descended from the English cavaliers.

But if we concede to every Virginian, not only his inherent gentility, but his unswerving purpose never to emigrate out of Slave territory, and an intuitive presentiment which pointed out which were to be the slave portions of adjacent Territories, by these same percentages of increase the 442,215 Virginian cavaliers of 1790 could be the progenitors of only 2,785,927 patricians to rally around the model cavalier of 1860—Jefferson Davis.

Lastly, in an estimate published in 1848 by Mr. Jesse Pickering, devoted entirely to the consideration of immigration as a national question, it is argued, with every appearance of truth, that in 1840 the foreign population of the Slave States was 1,177,965. But these must have displaced an equal number of the native born, and we should have only 3,426,908 of that class in 1840, 4,287,061 in 1850, and 5,311,668 in 1860, or in that case only five eights of the population could be of native descent, provided that not one emigrated. When we consider that the great immigration of all was between 1840 and 1860, we are forced to conclude that certainly not more than one half of the inhabitants of the present Confederate States can present the faintest claim to a descent from the citizens of 1790.

I think that few of my readers will now dispute that there is a physical impossibility of an unity of race among the Southerners, even had their emigrant forefathers been all of one nation. But they were of divers races even at the commencement. Let us examine each colony separately.

VIRGINIA.

Even Virginia was not entirely English. Barber's account of the State (p. 451) says of the valley of the Shenandoah:

"The eastern part of the valley being conveniently situated for emigrants from Pennsylvania, as well as from lower Virginia, the population there came to be a mixture of English Virginians and Germans and Scotch-Irish Presbyterians. The German Pennsylvanians, being passionate lovers of fat lands, no sooner heard of the rich valleys of the Shenando and its branches, than they began to join their countrymen from Europe in pouring themselves forth over the country above Winchester. Finding the main Shenando mostly preöccupied, they followed up the north and south branches on both sides of the Massanutten, or Peaked Mountain, until they filled up all the beautiful vales of the country for the space of sixty miles. So completely did they occupy the country, that the few stray English or Irish settlers among them did not sensibly affect the homogeneousness of the population."

And again:

"The first settlements of this portion of the valley were made by the Scotch Irish, with a few original Scotch among them. They settled in the neighborhoods around Martinsburg, in Berkely county, Winchester, and almost the entire counties of Orange and Guilford. The same race went on into North Carolina, and settled in the counties of Orange and Guilford, especially in the northern and middle parts of the latter county."

Beverley writes, (p. 228 :)

"The French refugees sent in thither by the charitable exhibition of his late majesty King William, are naturalized by a particular law for that purpose. In the year 1699 there went over about three hundred of these, and in the year following about two hundred more, and so on, till there arrived in all between seven and eight hundred men, women, and children, who had fled from France on account of their religion."

Bishop Meade (ii. 75) writes:

"That twelve Protestant German families, consisting of about fifty persons, arrived April 17th, in Virginia, and were therein settled near the Rappahannock river. That in 1717, seventeen Protestant German families, consisting of about fourscore persons, came and set down near their countrymen. And many more, both German and Swiss families, are likely to come there and settle likewise."

This report was made in 1720.

NORTH CAROLINA.

"The region south of Albermarle, as far down as Pamlico and Neuse, derived the larger part of its first settlers from the counties between the Sound and Virginia......As early as 1690, Martin informs us that some of the French Protestant refugees who had been sent by the royal benevolence to colonize on James River in Virginia, had purchased lands on Pamlico and planted themselves upon them.

In 1707 came a second body of French emigrants, considerable in numbers, from the James River settlement in Virginia. These had probably been allured by the representations of their countrymen who preceded them in 1690 and settled in Pamlico. This second migration proceeded beyond Pamlico, and made their home on Neuse and Trent rivers, whence, afterwards, some of them and of their descendants passed over into what are now Onslow and Carteret counties, where their names are still to be found. These last French emigrants, all Protestants, brought with them into Carolina their clergyman, Phillipe de Richebourg, some of whose descendants are still living in our county of Buncombe. After a time, he, with a portion of his people, proceeded farther south, and they planted themselves on the Santee River, where De Richebourg died.

Two or three years after this addition to the population, in the latter part of 1710, a considerable accession was made by the arrival of a large number of Germans and Swiss."

"The Germans were from Iiedelburg and its vicinity on the Neckar, in the Grand Duchy of Baden, and had been made the victims of religious persecution, because they could not change their creed with each successive change of their rulers." "It so happened that about the same time, Christopher, Baron de Graffenreid, a Swiss nobleman from Berne, was in England with a large number of his countrymen ; and they were anxious to emigrate to America.".... "A negotiation therefore commenced between these commissioners, the Swiss leaders, and the lords proprietors. The result was, that Graffenreid and Mitchell agreed to transport one hundred families of the palatines (about six hundred and fifty persons,) with their own Swiss colonists."

"In December, 1711, these German and Swiss landed at the confluence of the Neuse and Trent Rivers, and the town of New Berne was begun. There were now, therefore, about 1710, three classes of settlers in the state. First, there were the English, on the northern side of the Albemarle, gradually extending themselves westward beyond Chowan River. This was the most populous part of the province. Some of these people on Albemarle were also making their way southward toward Pamlico, and settling about Bath, while some probably halted in the intermediate region of Tyrrel.

Next there were the French Huguenots of the two emigrations from Virginia in 1690 and 1707. The first were on Pamlico, the last on Neuse, and chiefly on Trent River, whence some of them have wandered into what are Onslow and Carteret counties.

Lastly were the German palatines and Swiss. Of the former we know the number, six hundred and fifty ; of the latter there is no *certain* statement that we are aware of, though they are said in some documents we have seen, to have been fifteen hundred."

Hawks' North Carolina, ii, 849.

"A great number of French refugees were this year (1690) sent, at the King's expense, to the province of Virginia, and settled themselves on James river : others purchased land from the proprietors of Carolina and settled on Pamlico and Santee Rivers." Martin's History of North Carolina (New Orleans 1829) p. 192. Martin also mentions, p. 232-3, that French colonists from Virginia came in 1708, and further states, "besides a great number of palatines, fifteen hundred Swiss followed." In 1706 (p. 218)

"The population of the colony was composed of individuals of different nations, and consequently of various sects: Scotch Presbyterians, Dutch Lutherans, French Calvinists, Irish Catholics, English Churchmen, Quakers and Dissenters ; emigrants from Bermuda and the West Indies, which from their late settlement, could not be places remarkable for the education of young people in Christianity and morality."

In the appendix to his History is an account of the Moravians who settled in North Carolina.

SOUTH CAROLINA.

Mr. Pickett, whose history of Alabama was published at Charleston, S. C., in 1851, adds, "a company of forty Jews, acting under the broad principle of the charter, which gave freedom to all religions, save that of the Romish Church, landed at Savannah. Much dissatisfaction, both in England and America, arose in consequence of these Israelites, and Oglethorpe was solicited to send them immediately from the colony. He, however, generously permitted them to remain, which was one of the wisest acts of his life, for they and their descendants were highly instrumental in developing the commercial resources of this wild land." "The colony of Georgia had prospered under the wise guidance of Oglethorpe. The colonists, being from different nations, were various in their characters and religious creeds. Vaudois, Swiss, Piedmontese, Germans, Moravians, Jews from Portugal, Highlanders, English, and Italians were thrown together in this fine climate, new world, and new home."

"Round heads and cavaliers alike sought refuge in Carolina, which, for a long time, remained a pet province of the proprietors." *** "In 1674, when Nova Belgia, now New York, was conquered by the English, a number of the Dutch from that place sought refuge in Carolina. The proprietors facilitated their desire, and provided the ships which conveyed them to Charlestown. They were assigned lands on the southwest side of Ashley river, drew lots for their property, and founded a town which they called Jamestown, but which they afterwards deserted and spread themselves throughout the country, where they were joined by greater numbers from ancient Belgia.

Two vessels filled with foreign, perhaps French, protestants, were transported to Carolina, at the expense of

Charles II, in 1679 ; and the revocation of the edict of Nantz, a few years afterwards, by which the Huguenots were deprived of the only securities of life, liberty and fortune which their previous struggles had left them, contributed still more largely to the infant settlement, and provided Carolina with some of the noblest portions of her growing population." The History of South Carolina, by William Gilmore Simms. Charleston : 1840, pp. 58-9.

"Emigrants followed, though slowly, from Switzerland, Germany, and Holland ; and the Santee, the Congaree, the Wateree, and Edisto, now listened to the strange voices of several nations, who, in the old world, had hardly known each other except as foes." Ibid, p. 60.

About 1731, "a colony of Swiss settled on the Savannah and established the town of Purrysburgh. Eleven townships were marked out on various rivers." Ibid, p. 206.

"From this period (1761) we may date the true beginning not only of the prosperity, but the independence of Carolina...... Never did any colony flourish in a more surprising degree than South Carolina, as soon as the Cherokees were overcome, and the French and Spaniards driven from her borders. Multitudes of emigrants, from all parts of Europe, flocked to the interior, and pursuing the devious progress of the streams, sought out their sources, and planted their little colonies on the sides of lofty hills, or in the bosom of lovely vallies.

Six hundred poor German settlers arrived in one body; Ireland poured forth such numbers from her northern counties as almost threatened the depopulation of the kingdom. Scarce a ship sailed for any of the plantations that was not crowded with men, women and children, seeking the warm and fertile region of Carolina, of which such glowing tidings had reached their ears, and where the land was proffered in bounties to all new comers. Nor did the colony receive these accessions from Europe only. In the space of a single year, more than a thousand families with their effects, their cattle, hogs, and horses, crossed the Alleghanies from the eastern settlements and pitched their tents upon the Carolinean frontiers." Ibid, p. 121.

In Carroll's History of South Carolina (New York, 1836,) will be found a reprint of Dr. Hewit's Historical Account published in 1779. From it we make the following quotations :

P. 87. "The next acquisition America gained, was from the revocation of the edict of Nantz ; in consequence of which the flames of persecution broke out in France, and drove many of its best subjects out of that kingdom. These Protestant refugees were beneficial in many respects to England and Holland, and served greatly to promote the trade and manufactures of these nations. Among the other colonies in America which reaped advantage from this impolitic measure of France, Carolina had a larger share. Many of the Protestant refugees, having purchased lands from the proprietors, embarked with their families for that colony, and proved some of its best and most industrious inhabitants." P. 205. In 1715, "the Yemassees being expelled from Indian Land, the assembly passed two acts to appropriate those lands gained by conquest, for the use and encouragement of such of his majesty's subjects as should come over and settle upon them. Extracts of these acts being sent to England and Ireland and published among the people, five hundred men from Ireland transported themselves to Carolina, to take the benefit of them."

P. 295. In 1732, John Peter Perry, a native of Neufchatel in Switzerland, "having while in Carolina furnished himself with a flattering account of the soil and climate, and of the excellence and freedom of the provincial government, returned to Switzerland and published it among the people. Immediately one hundred and seventy poor Switzers agreed to follow him, and were transported to the fertile and delightful province as he described it ; and not long afterwards two hundred more came over and joined them."

P. 324. "By this time (1735) an account of the great privileges and indulgences granted by the crown for the encouragement of emigrants to Carolina, had been published through Britain and Ireland, and many industrious people in different parts had resolved to take the benefit of his majesty's bounty. Multitudes of labourers and husbandmen in Ireland, oppressed by landlords and bishops, and unable by their utmost diligence to procure a comfortable subsistence for their families, embarked for Carolina. The first colony of Irish people had lands granted them near Santee river, and formed the settlement called Williamsburg township."

P. 376. "The plan of settling townships, especially as it came accompanied with the royal bounty, had proved beneficial in many respects. It encouraged multitudes of poor oppressed people in Ireland, Holland and Germany to emigrate, by which means the province received a number of frugal and industrious settlers."

P. 485-7. In 1763, "one Stumpel, who had been an officer in the King of Prussia's service, being reduced at the peace, applied to the British ministry for a tract of land in America, and having got some encouragement, returned to Germany, where, by deceitful promises, he seduced between five and six hundred ignorant people from their native coun-country." He abandoned them in England, and having been supported by charity for a time, "his majesty, sensible that his colony of South Carolina had not its proportion of white inhabitants, and having expressed a particular attachment to it, signified his desire of transporting them to that province." Accordingly preparations were made, ships were furnished, and they landed at Charleston, in April, 1764.

P. 488. "Besides foreign Protestants, several persons from England and Scotland resorted to Carolina after the peace. *But of all other countries none has furnished the province with so many inhabitants as Ireland.* In the northern counties of that kingdom the spirit of emigration seized the people to such a degree, that it threatened almost a total depopulation. Such multitudes of husbandmen, labourers and manufacturers flocked over the Atlantic, that the landlords began to be alarmed, and concert ways and means for preventing the growing evil. Scarce a ship sailed for any of the plantations that was not crowded with men, women, and children. But the bounty allowed new settlers in Carolina proved a great encouragement, and induced numbers of these people, notwithstanding the severity of the climate, to resort to that province. The merchants, finding this bounty equivalent to the expenses of the passage, from avaricious motives persuaded the people to embark for Carolina, and often crammed such numbers of them into their ships that they were in danger of being stifled during the passage, and sometimes were landed in such a starved and sickly condition, that numbers of them died before they left Charleston.

Many causes may be assigned for this spirit of emigration that prevailed so much in Ireland: some, no doubt, emigrated from a natural restlessness of temper, and a desire of roving abroad, without any fixed object in view. Others were enticed over by flattering promises from their friends and relations, who had gone before them. But of other

causes of emigration, oppression at home was the most powerful and prevalent. Most men have a natural fondness
and partiality for their native country, and leave it with re-
luctance while they are able to earn a comfortable livelihood in it. That spot where they first drew the breath of
life, that society in which they spent the gay season of youth,
the religion, the manners and customs of those among
whom they were educated, all conspire to affect the heart,
and endear their native country to them. But poverty and
oppression will break through every natural tie and endear-
ment, and compel men to rove abroad in search of some
asylum against domestic hardships. Hence it happens that
many poor people forsook their native land, and preferred
the burning sky and unwholesome climate of Carolina, to
the temperate and mild air of their mother country. The
success that attended some friends who had gone before
them being also industriously published in Ireland, and
with all the exaggerations of travellers, gave vigor to the
spirit of adventure, and induced multitudes to follow their
countrymen, and run all hazards abroad, rather than starve
at home. Government winked at those emigrations, and
every year brought fresh strength to Carolina, insomuch
that the lands in Ireland were in danger of lying waste for
want of labourers, and the manufactures of dwindling into
nothing."

GEORGIA.

The records of the colonization of this state are more
imperfect than those of the Carolinas. It was emphatically
a pauper settlement. Its charter, dated in 1732, states that
"whereas we are credibly informed that many of our poor
subjects are through misfortunes and want of employment
reduced to great necessity, insomuch as by their labour they
are not able to provide a maintenance for themselves and
families; and if they had means to defray their charges of
passage, and other expenses incident to new settlements,
they would be glad to settle in any of our provinces in
America;" therefore certain lands were granted to a Cor-
poration.

In a tract published in 1741, and reprinted in the Georgia Historical Collections, ii, 305, it is shown that in eight
years ending 9th June, 1740, 1,521 persons had been sent

over on the charity, whereof 915 were British and 606 foreign. The same tract, ii, 308, says about twenty miles further up the river is the town of Ebenezer, where the Salsburgers are settled, with two ministers, one of whom computed that the number of his congregation in June 1738 consisted of one hundred and forty six. . . . At their desire another embarkation of their countrymen, who are willing to go from Germany and join them, is designed to be sent for with all convenient speed.

"In the southern part of the province is the town of New Inverness, where the Highlanders are settled."

A letter from Thomas Coram, dated 1734, (Georgia Hist. Coll. ii, 971,) says, "But I beg leave to say something of the Jews, who to the number of between forty and fifty have procured themselves to be already settled there contrary to the will, and without the consent of the trustees, and there are more of their nation now going over to them. I humbly conceive these shocking matters require your most serious attention; for unless you speedily take some vigorous resolutions to suppress effectually the two great evils aforesaid, Georgia will soon become a Jewish colony."

Hewitt's account, already cited, (Carroll's History of S. Carolina i, 310,) says, " But after the representation and memorial from the legislature of Carolina reached Britain, the nation considerd Georgia to be of the utmost importance to the British settlements in America, and began to make still more vigorous efforts for its speedy population. The first embarkations of poor people from England, being collected from towns and cities, were found equally idle and useless members of society abroad, as they had been at home. A hardy and bold race of men, inured to rural labour and fatigue, they were persuaded would be much better adapted both for cultivation and defence. To find men possessed of these qualifications, the trustees turned their eyes to Germany and the Highlands of Scotland, and resolved to send over a number of Scotch and German labourers to their infant province. When they published their terms at Inverness, a hundred and thirty Highlanders immediately accepted them, and were transported to Georgia. A township on the river Altamaha, which was considered as the boundary between the British and Spanish territories, was allotted for the Highlanders, on which dangerous situation they settled, and built a town which they called New Inverness. About the same time a hundred and seventy Germans embarked with James Oglethorpe and were fixed in another quarter, so that in the space of three years, Georgia received above four hundred British subjects, and about one hundred and seventy foreigners. Afterwards several adventurers, both from Scotland and Germany, followed their countrymen, and added further strength to the province, and the trustees flattered themselves with the hopes of soon seeing it in a promising condition."

In White's Historical Collections of Georgia, (New York, 1855,) p. 37, is a list of grants of land from 1741—1754. Without attempting an exact analysis, it is evident that not one fourth can be considered English names. The German and Scotch names constitute by far the greater portion.

White's Statistics of Georgia, (Savannah, 1849) mentions, p. 96, the arrival of the Germans in 1733 and their settlement at Ebenezer, and page 101, the settlement of Jews at Savannah.

Such an array of authorities ought to be conclusive against any idea that England has been the fountain head, even of that portion which may be considered as descended from the early colonists. Even Africa has a certain undeniable claim.

In 1853, a memoir of James Fontaine was published, accompanied by letters from members of his family. He was a Huguenot, who had settled in Virginia, and his descendants have been among the most distinguished of her citizens.

The letters of his sons to relatives in England are very instructive. I quote from one from Peter Fontaine, dated March 2, 1756, in which he regrets that the English had not intermarried with the Indians:

"But here methinks I can hear you observe, 'What! Englishmen intermarry with Indians?' But I can convince you that they are guilty of much more heinous practices, more unjustifiable in the sight of God and man (if that indeed may be called a bad practice;) for many base wretches among us take up with negro women, by which means the country swarms with mulatto bastards; and these mulattoes, if but three generations removed from the black father or mother, may, by the indulgence of the laws of the country, intermarry with the white people, *and actually do every day so marry.*"

This is the testimony of a Virginian gentleman, made a century ago; I do not care to more than point to the possible infusion of other than English blood into the veins of the gentlemen who desire to adopt the Cavalier as their national device.

Farther than this, we read in Wirt's life of Patrick Henry, (ed. 1818 p. 241,) that in 1784 Patrick Henry proposed a bill which passed through two readings, entitled "a Bill for the encouragement of marriages with the Indians," which proposed a bounty to every free white male who would marry an Indian female of lawful age, or any free female who would marry with any male Indian of lawful age, and enacting "that the offspring of the intermarriages aforesaid shall be entitled, in all respects, to the same rights and privileges, under the laws of this commonwealth, as if they had proceeded from intermarriages among free white inhabitants thereof."

It is not necessary to inquire what percentage of Indian or Negro blood may be found in the free population of the Southern States; it is evident that the purity of lineage so essential to a race of gentlemen, has been often imperilled since the first colonists landed here.

SOCIAL STATUS OF THE ENGLISH COLONISTS.

We now proceed to examine the social position, prior to the emigration, of those Englishmen who did in a certain degree colonize the present Slave States, and in a much greater degree colonize New England. I must confess having long wondered at the persistent statement of Englishmen that the citizens of the United States were the offspring of the vagabonds and felons of Europe. Having examined the history of the families of New England with much interest, and finding therein no confirmation of this idea, I had held it but the outbreak of prejudice and ignorance. Yet since the present rebellion has caused so much inquiry into the antecedents of the Southerners, I find that the assertion is well fou.ided, but that it concerns those who have hitherto been loudest in their claims to a distinguished ancestry. The citations may perhaps be best examined by arranging them under the names of the several colonies.

NORTH CAROLINA.

"There was also a third class of labourers whom our records show to have been in the colony. These were white men, English convicts transported to America for their crimes. . . . Exile was first introduced as a punishment in English law, in the reign of Elizabeth, anno 1596. It was then enacted that "such rogues as were dangerous to the inferior people, should be banished the realm. James I virtually converted this into an act for transportation to America, without any aid from parliament, and, by the mere exercise of his own will. He wrote a letter, in 1619, to the treasurer and council of Virginia, (residing in London,) commanding them "to send a hundred dissolute persons to Virginia, which the Knight Marshal would deliver to them for that purpose." The first English Statute which uses the word "transport," was passed in 18 Charles II (1666.) This gives a power to the judges at their discretion either "to execute or transport to America for life the moss-troopers of Cumberland and Northumberland. Until the reign of George I, this mode of punishment was but little used. By statutes passed in the fourth and sixth years of that King (1718 and 1720,) the courts were authorized to order any felons who were entitled to their clergy, on conviction, to be transported to the American plantations; and after these enactments the practice became common enough. The colonies to which they were sent were New York, New Jersey, Pennsylvania, Delaware, Maryland, Virginia, North and South Carolina, and after 1733, to Georgia. The whole number sent is estimated by Lang (in his History of Transportation,) at fifty thousand. But this emptying of the jails of England upon America did not pass without remonstrance from the colonies, and formed one of the serious complaints set forth in the enumeration of our grievances at the time of the Revolution; for England never discontinued the practice until we had achieved our independence."

"The plan of transportation was this : Owners and captains of vessels conracted to carry the convicts; and as remuneration for the service, agreed, on their arrival, to sell them to the planters for the times named in their respective sentences. Lang tells us that these transported felons, male and female, were bought by the planters for the terms specified in their respective warrants, and worked with the negro slaves under the lash of an overseer."

We have seen in the chapter on laws, the extent of the master's powers and the convict's privileges. So common and well understood was the practice of selling convicts into colonial slavery, that one of the most remarkable of England's writers of fiction, who lived at the time, availed himself of the existing custom to build on it one of the most startling incidents of his story; and the "Moll Flanders" of Defoe presents a picture of convicts transported to Virginia, which, drawn from events around him, is sketched, according to his custom, with minute accuracy of detail, and wants no additional touch to improve its verisimilitude. As to the criminals themselves, their condition was varied according to circumstances. If they or their relations were possessed of wealth, they had but to offer the captain a higher price for themselves than he could get when he reached America, and exposed them in market overt, and then they never went into bondage nor were ever made the subject of a bid. Sometimes too, when they were poor, and consequently sold, they found a stimulus to seek the improvement of their condition, and emerged from their degraded position.

An old writer, in speaking of Virginia, thus describes them : 'They go there poor, and come back rich; there they plant, trade, thrive and increase; even your transported felons, sent to Virginia instead of Tyburn, thousands of them, if we are not misinformed, have, by turning their hands to industry and improvement, and, which is best of all, to honesty, become rich, substantial planters and merchants, settled large families and been famous in the country ; nay, we have seen many of them made magistrates, officers of militia, captains of good ships, and masters of good estates.*

But sometimes the owners and masters of ships did

---

* Posthethwayte's Dict. of Commerce, vol. ii, p. 319. The Herald's office, which (it is well known) preserves with great care the *genuine aristocracy* of America, can doubtless furnish a list of these felons thus converted into gentlemen. They must by no means be confounded with the "first families" of the country, who never thus stole into notoriety.— *Dr. Hawks' note.*

not wait for the sentence of the law to furnish them with a cargo. The picture of society in the ports of England at that day brings to our notice, and especially in London, the habit of kidnapping those convicted of no crime, but who, found perchance in a moment of drunkenness, or overcome, if sober, by brute force, were hurried on board the vessel ready to depart, and presently found themselves exposed to sale as slaves in some one of the American plantations. Children were stolen and sent over.

The planter was much too discreet to ask troublesome questions, and the captain, of course, told what lies he pleased. Another, but small class of temporary white bondmen was to be found in those who were bound as apprentices, both in England and in the provinces; these, however, were mostly employed as house-servants, or trained to mechanical arts, and had but little employment in agriculture. The purchased convicts and negro slaves encountered the harder toil of clearing and cultivating the lands."

Hawks' Hist. of North Carolina, (Fayetteville, N. C., 1858,) ii, 230.

"We fear that our previous chapters will not have accomplished one of the purposes for which they were written, if they have not enabled the reader, before reaching this page, to form for himself a tolerably accurate picture of the general manners of the different classes that compose the society of the proprietary times.

We say different classes, because the artificial distinctions of society were prominent enough. There were educated men in the province, some of whom were natives, who had been sent in early life for training in English schools and universities. They had returned about the period of incipient manhood, and brought with them the refinements and habits belonging to the class of educated gentry in England, with which they had so long associated. There were also those who, not native, had come in maturer age with similiar tastes and corresponding cultivation. Some of these were allied also to families of rank in England, and added pride of blood to the courtesies of gentle breeding. There was material therefore for a quasi aristocracy, which however was not numerous.

Martin's History of North Carolina, i, 279 and ii, 48-9, treats very fully both of the foreigners and convicts.

Next there was a class which by shrewdness, thrift and superior intelligence, had contrived to become rich, while the masses remained poor; and who, rising gradually as their accumulation increased, had become large landed proprietors, in possession of some of the best bodies of land in the country, the future value of which they had the sagacity to foresee when they came to the province in its infancy........It was out of this class that the lord proprietors usually selected their deputies, thus making them members of the council, and elevating them to a level with those who constituted the pseudo-aristocracy to which we have referred.

The next class who were freemen, was composed of the ordinary and uninstructed, who, in England, would have belonged to the peasantry or agricultural laborers, some of whom had voluntarily emigrated, and were employed on the farms where they labored for wages. There were, however, others among this class whose crimes had reduced them to a temporary slavery: these were the transported convicts, male and female, who had been brought in and sold to the planters........This bondage possessed, however, one redeeming feature—the slavery was temporary; and at its close, the emancipated bondsman was furnished with both lands and tools, and might become the founder of a new family and a new character.

If his conduct as a servant were marked by submission and fidelity, his burdens were somewhat lightened in his progress to freedom, and the sympathies of a generous and pitying master were sometimes enlisted in his encouragement and aid, when he began the hard, but not hopeless task of obtaining a new name, and acquiring property on which he could look without the humiliating consciousness that he had obtained it by crime.

It is of little consequence to inquire what families now deservedly respectable, in the old provinces where convicts were most numerous, had an origin as humble as this. That some did, is certain."

Hawks' North Carolina, ii, 572-3.

1703. "Among the first emigrants, some sense of religion had been for a while preserved, but the next generation, reared in a wilderness where divine service was hardly ever performed, and where private devotions cannot be supposed to have been much attended to, were rather remarkable for loose, licentious principles, and the fundamental principles of the christian religion were often treated with the ridicule and contempt of professed infidelity. The population of the colony was composed of individuals of different nations, and consequently of various sects: Scotch Presbyterians, Dutch Lutherans, French Calvinists, Irish Catholics, English Churchmen, Quakers and Dissenters; emigrants from Bermuda and the West Indies, which, from their late settlements, could not be places remarkable for the education of young people, in Christianity and morality."

Martins' History of North Carolina (New Orleans: 1829) i, 218.

GEORGIA.

The original plan of Oglethorpe was "to provide an asylum or place of refuge for the honest industrious poor, and the unfortunate, with some view to the relief of the persecuted Protestants in Germany. Among these unfortunate persons it could not be guarded against that numbers, unfortunate only by their own vices or follies, intruded themselves among the real objects of charity." We have already shown that the foreign element in the population was very large. It is clear that the English portion was not from the gentry but the paupers;—not from the manor-house, but from the jail and poor-house. There were several sermons delivered 1732-1745 before the Society in London, of Trustees for establishing the Colony of Georgia. The following is an extract from one by Rev. George Watts, London, 1736:

"And this is a farther excellence of this DESIGN, that it saves many distressed people of our own, from want and destruction........The fact I think is plain, that there are numbers of people that want employment, and numbers more that cannot subsist on the employment they have. Hence it is that our roads are infested, and our streets thronged with wretched creatures, forced to seek a livelihood from vice and wickedness, and living only to corrupt others. Hence it is that our prisons are full of miserable men, useless to all the purposes of society whilst they are *there*, and by too long a restraint, made useless likewise when they came out........Surely they are still objects of such a charity (if any one can be found) that shall relieve their distress, and cure their idleness and extravagance at the same time. What shall we do then with these miserable, useless or pernicious inhabitants?

Thus shall we erect a new Kingdom to ourselves, out of the refuse of our own people, and the subjects of neighboring nations.

If ever, therefore, there was in reality a colony, what it should be by description, a refuge to the poor, and ease and security to the rich, a nursery of people, and a supply of necessaries, a reward to the deserving, and a reformation to the disorderly; this, of all others, seems most likely to answer such a character."

Again a sermon by Rev. James King, in 1743 pursues the same theme of aid to the poor, and refers to a vote of the House of Commons, 29 June, 1742, providing for the transportation of paupers by means of this society. At p. 21, the author writes, "many families of our own poor have already settled there; and they have been joined by the indigent protestants of other countries, who have resorted hither to supply the exigences both of their bodies and their souls."

VIRGINIA.

As the most conspicuous claimant of a Cavalier origin, let Virginia have the benefit of most extensive quotations. I give the first place to an authority who contrasts Virginia with New England.

"It is certain that the first settlers of New England did not (as in some of our Colonies) come over indigent or criminals, but as devout religious Puritans; they were not servants to the adventurers as in some Colonies." (Douglas* vol 1, part ii, 371.)

"The settling of our sundry Colonies, have been upon several Occasions and from various Beginnings. New England was first settled by people from England, tenacious of their own non-conformist way of Religious Worship, were resolved to endure any Hardships, viz: a very distant Removal, Inclemencies of the Climate, Barrenness of the soil &c., in Order to enjoy their own Way of Thinking, called Gospel-Privileges, in Peace and Purity. Our West India

---

* A summary Historical and Political, of the first planting, progressive Improvements and present state of the British settlements in North America. By William Douglas, M. D. Boston, N. E. 1749.

Islands have been settled or increased, some of them by Royalists, some by Parliamentarians, some by Tories, some by Whigs, at different Times Fugitives or Exiles from their native Country. Virginia and Maryland have been for many Years and continue to be a sink for transported Criminals. Pennsylvania being the property of Mr. Penn, a Quaker, he planted it with Quakers, (as Lord Baltimore for the same Reason at first planted Maryland with Roman Catholics) it is lately very much increased by Husbandmen swarming from Ireland and Germany." Douglas, vol. 1, part i, 115.

"The assiduous and well-qualified Agent, Dummer, in his ingenious and politick Piece published in London, 1721, writes 'That the expense of settling the Massachusetts Bay Colony for the first twelve years, was about 200,000£ sterling; that the settlers are neither necessitous nor Criminals'." Douglass, vol. I, part ii, 428.

"Our Plantations in America, New England excepted, have been generally settled, 1. By Malcontents with the Administrations from Time to Time; 2. By fraudulent Debtors, as a refuge from their Creditors; and by Convicts or Criminals, who chose Transportation rather than Death." Douglass, vol. I, part ii, 490.

VIRGINIA — CAMPBELL'S HISTORY.

1619. "The condition of the white servants of the colony, many of them convicts, was so abject that men accustomed to see their own race in bondage could look with more indifference at the worse condition of the slaves." p. 145.

1619. "The planters at length enjoyed the blessings of property and the society of women. The wives (90) were sold to the colonists for one hundred and twenty pounds of tobacco.... The price of a wife afterwards became higher."

1620. "One hundred disorderly persons or convicts sent over during the previous year by the King's order were employed as servants."

1621. Commercial letter. "We send you a shipment, one widow and eleven maids for wives for the people of Virginia; there hath been especial care in the choice of them. There are nearly fifty more that are shortly to come."

1617—22. "Nor were these settlers voluntary emigrants; the bulk of them had been sent over without regard to their choice by the King or the Virginia Company."

1618. "There came yearly to trade above thirty vessels. Many of the masters and chief mariners of these vessels had plantations, houses, and servants in the Colony."

1660. "A good many republicans and puritans had
found their way to Virginia."

1661. The failure of the schemes proposed in the
Virginia Assembly, for the establishment of towns, is attrib-
uted by the author of "Virginia's Cure," to the majority of
the House of Burgesses *who are said to have come over at first
as servants,* and who although they may have accumulated by
their industry competent estates, yet owing to their mean
education, were incompetent to judge of public matters, either in church or state."

1670. "In the year 1670, complaints were made to
the General Court by members of the Council and others
being gentlemen of the counties of York, Gloucester and
Middlesex, representing their apprehensions of danger from
the great number of felons and other dangerous villains,
sent hither from the prisons of England. Masters of vessels were prohibited from landing any such convicts or jail-
birds."

1671. "Captains Bristow and Walbier were required
to give security in the sum of one million pounds of tobacco and cash that Mr. Nevett should send out the Newgate-
birds within two months."

Mr. Jefferson has made the following remark :—"The
malefactors sent to America were not sufficient in number to merit enumeration as one class out of three which
peopled America. It was at a late period of their history
that the practice begun. I have no book by me which ena-
bles me to point out the date of its commencement, but I
do not think the whole number sent would amount to two
thousand," and he supposed they and their descendants did
not in 1786, exceed four thousand, "which is little more
than one thousandth part of the whole population." Mr.
Jefferson appears to have been mistaken in his opinion that
malefactors were not sent over until a late period in the an-
nals of Virginia; and he probably underrated the number of
their descendants." Campbell, p. 270.

1670. Population 40,000 of which 2,000 were negro
slaves, and 6,000 white servants.

"Three kinds of servants are brought over. First,
such as came upon certain wages by agreement for a certain

time. Second, such as are bound by indentures, commonly called *Kids*, who are usually to serve four or five years, and third, those convicts or felons that are transported, whose room they had much rather have than their company. These are to serve seven and sometimes fourteen years.... To prevent too great a stock of which servants and negroes, many attempts and laws have been in vain made.... They afterwards rent a small plantation or else turn overseers." Hugh Jones, Present State of Virginia, (1724,) p. 54.

"But for the generality, the servants and inferior sort of persons, who have either been sent over to Virginia or have transported themselves thither, have been and are the poorest, idlest and worst of mankind, the refuse of Great Britain and Ireland, and the outcast of the people." Ibid. p. 114.

———

"The country is reported to be an unhealthy place, a nest of rogues, whores, dissolute and rooking persons; a place of intolerable labour, bad usage and hard diet. To answer these several calumnies, I shall first show what it was, next what it is. At the first settling, and many years after, it deserved most of these aspersions, (nor were they aspersions but truths).... Then were jails emptied, youths seduced, infamous women drilled in.... no redress of grievances, complaints paid with stripes.... Yet was not Virginia all this while without divers honest and virtuous inhabitants." John Hammond's "Leah and Rachel," London, 1656.

Robert Beverly (I quote from the edition published at Richmond in 1855) says:

"Those that went over to that country first, were chiefly single men who had not the incumbrance of wives and children in England; and if they had, they did not expose them to the fatigue and hazard of so long a voyage, until they saw how it should fare with themselves. From hence it came to pass, that when they were settled there in a comfortable way of subsisting a family, they grew sensible of the misfortune of wanting wives, and such as had left wives in England sent for them, but the single men were put to their shifts. They excepted against the Indian women on account of their being pagans, as well as their complexions. and for fear they should conspire with those of their own nation to destroy their husbands. Under this difficulty they had no hopes but that the plenty in which they lived might invite modest women, of small fortunes, to go over thither from England. However, they would not receive any but such as could carry sufficient certificate of their modesty and good behavior. Those, if they were but moderately qualified in all other respects, might depend upon marrying very well in those days, without any fortune. Nay, the first planters were so far from expecting money with a woman, that 'twas a common thing for them to buy a deserving wife that carried good testimonials of her character, at the price of one hundred pounds, and make themselves believe they had a bargain.

"§ 67. But this way of peopling the colony was only at first. For after the advantages of the climate and the fruitfulness of the soil were well known, and all the dangers incident to infant settlements were over, people of better condition retired thither with their families, either to increase the estates they had before, or to avoid being persecuted for their principles of religion or government.

"Thus in the time of the rebellion in England, *several* good cavalier families went thither with their effects to escape the tyranny of the usurper, or acknowledgment of his title. And so again, upon the Restoration, many people of the opposite party took refuge there, to shelter themselves from the king's resentment. But Virginia had not many of these last, because that country was famous for holding out the longest for the royal family of any of the English dominions.* For which reason the Roundheads went, for the most part, to New England, as did most of those that in the reign of King Charles II were molested on account of their religion, though some of these fell likewise to the share of Virginia.

As for malefactors condemned to transportation, though the greedy planter will always buy them, yet it is to be feared they will be very injurious to the country, which has already suffered many murders and robberies, the effect of that new law of England.

1619. "One hundred idle and dissolute persons in custody for various misdemeanors, were transported by authority of the King and against the wishes of the company to Virginia....At the accession of Sir Edwin to office, after twelve years labor, and an expenditure of eighty thous-

*Yet our author had already shown that Dennis, Cromwell's captain, 'contrived a stratagem which betrayed the country. He had got a considerable parcel of goods aboard, which belonged to two of the Council, and found a method of informing them of it. By this means they were reduced to the dilemma, either of submitting or losing their goods. This caused factions amongst them, so that at last'—we blush to add—'the colony surrendered— and saved the goods.' *En dat Virginia quintum.* The fifth crown had its price even for a 'usurper.'

and pounds by the company, there were in the colony no more than six hundred persons, men, women, and children. In one year he provided a passage for twelve hundred and sixty one new emigrants. Among these were ninety agreeable young women, poor but respectable and incorrupt, to furnish wives to the colonists. . . . This new commodity was transported at the expense of the colony and sold to the young planters, and the following year another consignment was made of sixty young maids of virtuous education, young, handsome and well recommended. A wife in the first lot sold generally for one hundred pounds of tobacco, but as the value of the new article became known in the market, the price rose, and a wife would bring a hundred and fifty pounds of tobacco. A debt for a wife was of a higher dignity than other debts, and to be paid first." *Gazeteer of Virginia.*

Beverly notes also about these servants that "a white woman is rarely or never put to work in the ground, if she be good for anything else."

Bishop Meade (vol. i, p. 89) speaks also of these female servants:

"While the company and the Governor were endeavoring to improve the condition of the colony, by selecting a hundred young females of good character to be wives to the laborers on the farms of Virginia, King James had determined to make of the colony a Botany Bay for the wretched convicts in England, and ordered one hundred to be sent over. The company remonstrated, but in vain. A large portion, if not all of them, were actually sent. The influence of this must have been pernicious. Whether it was continued by his successors, and how long, and to what extent, I know not."

And again (pp. 365 — '6), he says:

"The greatest difficulty they (the vestrymen) appear to have had, was with the hired servants, of whom, at an early period, great numbers came over to this country binding themselves to the richer families. The number of illegitimate children born of them and thrown upon the parish, led to much action on the part of the legislature. *The lower order of persons in Virginia, in a great measure, sprang from these apprenticed servants and from poor exiled culprits.*"

Stith says, (ed. 1747, p. 103), under date of 1609:

"But a great part of this new company consisted of un-

ruly sparks, packed off by their friends to escape worse des-
tinies at home. And the rest were chiefly made up of poor
gentlemen, broken tradesmen, rakes, and libertines, footmen,
and such others as were much fitter to spoil or ruin a commonwealth, than to help to raise or maintain one".

Again, (p. 306), in describing one of the domestic quar-
rels of the colony, he copies a statement:

"And whereas it was affirmed that very few of his majesty's servants were lost in those days, and those persons of
the meanest rank, they replied that for one that then died
five had perished in Sir Thomas Smith's time, many being of
ancient houses, and born to estates of a thousand pounds a
year, some more, some less,who likewise perished by famine."

These extracts are all that I can urge in support of the
claim of Virginians to be descended from the English gentry.
There may be many other authorities; it is for the asserters
of this theory to produce them, and I certainly would repub-
lish them if I could obtain them.

I regret exceedingly that I am unable to present any
complete statement of the number of convicts transported
from Great Britain to the colonies, with the report of their
destination. Such records, no doubt, exist in England, and
can be obtained if any one be bold enough to challenge farther
inquiry. I am able to give a general idea of the extent of
the custom, by copying the notices made monthly among the
"Current Events" of the Annual Register and the London
Magazine.

These lists are imperfect, since the account is mainly
for the sessions at the Old Bailey, and is not continuous and
full even for these. We see many indications that the other
courts in Great Britain sentenced many felons, and that the
place of punishment was almost invariably Virginia, Maryland, or the Carolinas.

I believe I am correct in saying that the term "the Plantations in America," was applied exclusively to our Southern
states, and did not include any of the West India Islands.

In December 1717, there were 27 sentenced at the Old
Bailey to transportation. In 1718, 137; in 1719, 184; in
1720, 173; in 1721, 200; in 1722, 182; in 1723, 219; in
1724, 226; in 1725, 290; in 1726, 234; in 1727, 187.

These are by no means perfect lists, being only for various months in each year, and only for the session at the Old Bailey. The disposal of the convicts is shown by notes like these: "August 1718, 106 convicts that were ordered for transportation, were taken out of Newgate, and put into a lighter, at Black fryers stairs; from whence they were carried through Bridge to Long Reach, and then shipped on board the Eagle Galley, Captain Staples, Commander, bound to *Virginia and Maryland.*"

"May 1719, 105 felons convict taken out of Newgate, the Marshalsea, and several other country gaols, were put on ship-board, to be transported to Maryland." "May 1720, 92 felons convict out of Newgate, and 62 out of the Marshalsea, were put on ship-board to be transported to Virginia." February, 1723, 36 felons convict were taken out of Newgate, and conveyed on ship-board, in order to be transported to Maryland." 1724, 5 & 6. " Convict felons shipped to the Plantations in America."

I find among the items of monthly intelligence in the *London Magazine,* the records of felons sentenced to transportation to his majesty's plantations in America, and often the different colonies named. I find a calculation incidentally made, about 1750, that 500 culprits were hung annually in Great Britain—and bloody as the circuits then were, I cannot believe that less than ten times that number annually received the questionable charity of expatriation. I will give a few extracts, to show the foundation upon which Southern society has been erected.

In October, 1732, "68 men and 50 women, felons convict, were carried from Newgate to Black Fryars, and put on board a lighter, to be carried down the river, to be shipped on board the Cæsar, off of Deptford, for transportation to Virginia." January, 1736: "This morning 140 felons convict for transportation, were carried from Newgate, and shipped for the plantations, and 18 likewise from the new gaol at Southwark." In May, 106 were also so shipped. In 1738, 126 were shipped at one time "for the plantations." In 1739, 127 were shipped "to America." In 1741, 9 of the felons on board a ship lying at Blackwall, "to be transported to Virginia," made a bold dash to escape.

In May 1747, " We are informed that several large ships sailed lately from Liverpool, with the rebel prisoners, under strong convoy to Virginia and Maryland, and other of his majesty's plantations, which makes the whole of what have been transported, upward of 1,000." In January, 1749, " the "Laura " with 135 convicts, bound to Maryland, was cast away." In 1754, Mr. Stuart was the contractor to transport convicts "to America." In 1758, "63 men and women transports were sent from Newgate on board the ship " Trial," bound to Maryland, and 45 from the new gaol, Southwark." Later in the same year, 53 "for America "— 36 men and 20 women "for the plantations." In 1761, a ship sails with 8 men and 27 women "convicts to America." In October, "27 women and 18 men from Newgate, 14 from the new gaol, and 62 from the country goals, were transported to America this month." In 1762, 36 women and 5 men convicts were shipped "to America;" "62 convicts were embarked for Maryland."

In 1776, I find : "The above observation occurred to my mind a few days ago, on seeing the convicts pass along to the water side, in order to be shipped for America, with fifes playing before them, "Through the wood, laddie,"—an evidence that the practice was then in force, and a matter of course.

In a "Tour through the British Plantations," published in the London Magazine, in 1755, which contains a good account of each colony, I read of Virginia, that under Sir Edwyn Sandys, "there were 12,000 acres laid off for the use of the company, and 100 tenants or planters sent to be placed thereon ; and 3,000 acres for the support of the Governor, for the planting of which, 100 more men were sent; and what was now become absolutely necessary, there were no less than 90 young women, of a healthful constitution, and unspotted reputation, sent out to be married to the planters, instead of diseased and profligate strumpets, *as is now* the ridiculous practice. . . . Thus the company and colony began to be in a thriving way : but now they began to be oppressed by the Government here, for in November, they were ordered to send over to Virginia, at their own charge, 100 felons or vagabonds, then it may be supposed in prison, which they were obliged to comply with."

The same writer says of Maryland:

"The convicts that are transported here, sometimes prove very worthy creatures, and entirely forsake their former follies; but the trade has for some time run in another channel; and so many volunteer servants come over, especially Irish, that the other is a commodity much blown over. Several of the best planters, or their ancestors, have, in the two colonies,* been originally of the convict class, and therefore are much to be praised and esteemed for forsaking their old courses."

In 1751, (p. 293) is printed the following:

"A LETTER LATELY PUBLISHED IN VIRGINIA."

"SIR: When we see our papers filled continually, with accounts of the most audacious robberies, the most cruel murders, and infinite other atrocities, perpetrated by convicts transported from Europe, what melancholy, what terrible reflections must it occasion! What will become of our posterity? These are some of thy favors, Britain! Thou art called our mother country; but what good mother ever sent thieves and villains to accompany her children; to corrupt some with their infectious vices, and murder the rest? What father ever endeavored to spread the plague in his family! We do not ask fish, but thou givest us serpents! In what can Britain show a more sovereign contempt for us, than by emptying their gaols into our settlements, unless they would likewise empty their offal upon our tables? What must we think of that board, which has advised the repeal of every law we have hitherto made to prevent this deluge of wickedness overwhelming us; and with this cruel sarcasm, that these laws were against the public utility, for they tended to prevent the improvement and well peopling of the colonies! And what must we think of those merchants, who for the sake of a little paltry gain, will be concerned in importing and disposing of these abominable cargoes?"

I can hardly believe that my readers will require any further proofs, that the idea that the inhabitants of the Seceding States are descended from the English Cavaliers, is entirely erroneous.

When we descend from the lofty realms of fancy, in which these Southern enthusiasts dwell, and seek to discover

---

* Virginia was the other, of which he was writing.

what proportion, however small, of truth there is in the story, we are almost unable to detect it. Genealogy is a science, based upon facts. Certain records, such as the official list of births, deaths, and marriages, preserved on town, county, state or parish records, and, in some cases, private memoranda, are the only recognized authorities. In New England these records have been kept with remarkable accuracy, since the commencement of the settlement. In Virginia, and probably in the other Southern States, these records are wanting. As is shown by Bishop Meade in his book, especially devoted to the history of the "Old Churches and Old Families of Virginia," the records of the parishes have been lost, the churchyards destroyed, and few authorities, save tradition, remain. Even in the case of the Washingtons, a family whose records have been traced with sedulous care, there is now no evidence of the connections with an English family, sufficient to satisfy Heralds College. In short there are two hundred families in Massachusetts having as great a claim, through traditions and the use of coats-of-arms, to the rank of gentlemen, as the bulk of the patrician families of Virginia.

We have therefore to glean here and there, little fragments of truth, to prevent our styling the entire claim of the Cavaliers, a bold fabrication. A very few Virginia families can be thus proved to have sprung from the English gentry. The book of Bishop Meade's, already cited, gives the following meagre list, and any other authorities are still wanting. He names the families of Ambler, Barradall, Baylor, Bushrod, Burwell, Carter, Digges, Fairfax, Fitzhugh, Fowke, Harrison, Jacqueline, Lee, Lewis, Ludwell, Mason, Robinson, Spottswood, Sandys, and Washington. I believe I have omitted none, and I have rather strained a point in admitting some.

I do not, of course, mean to deny that others may exist, but until the proofs are submitted to examination, there is no justice in presuming them to exist.

I quote from Wirt's Life of Patrick Henry, the following description of Virginian society by "a gentleman who lived in those days, (1768) and who had the best opportunities of judging on the subject:"

"There were then, first aristocrats, composed of the great landholders, who had settled themselves below tide water on the main rivers, and lived in a style of luxury and extravagance, insupportable by the other inhabitants, and which indeed ended in several instances, in the ruin of their fortunes. Next to these were what might be called *half-breeds;* the descendants of the younger sons and daughters of the aristocrats, who inherited the pride of their ancestors, without their wealth.

Then came the pretenders, men who from vanity or the impulse of growing wealth, or from that enterprise which is natural to talents, sought to detach themselves from the plebeian ranks, to which they properly belonged, and imitated at some distance, the manners and habits of the great. Next to these were a solid and independent yeomanry, looking askance at those above, yet not venturing to jostle them. And last and lowest, a *feculum* of beings called overseers, the most abject, degraded, unprincipled race ; always cap in hand to the dons who employed them, and furnishing material for the exercise of their pride, insolence, and spirit of domination.

Does this picture suggest a colony composed entirely of gentry or "First Families"?

Again, it is often most erroneously supposed, that the names of certain families is a proof of their gentle origin. This idea is wholly unfounded. The gentry of England consist of certain families, whose ancestors held a certain rank. Unless the line of descent can be clearly proved, identity of name signifies nothing. We are arguing in this essay, upon a certain arbitrary nomenclature, and we are bound by certain well-known rules. A Courtenay, a Howard, a De Vere, is not a gentleman in the sense the heralds use the term, unless he can trace his pedigree. Yet even here, the Virginians have no exclusive claim. The following list is given by Bishop Meade, as comprising the chief familes of the Virginian gentry.

"Names of some of the Old and Leading Families in Eastern Virginia, in Colonial Times and immediately succeding the Revolution.—(*Meade*, ii, 428.)

Allen, Alexander, Ambler, Archer, Armistead, Atkinson, Aylett, Acril.

Bacon, Baker, Ball, Baldwin, Ballard, Bankhead, Banister, Bassett, Baylor, Baynham, Berkeley, Beverly, Birchett, Blair, Bland, Bolling, Bouldin, Booth, Bowyer, Bradley, Brent, Braxton, Bowdoin, Browne, Brooke, Broadnaxe, Burwell, Burley, Butler, Buckner, Byrd, Baskerville, Branch, Booker, Blow.

Cabell, Calloway, Carr, Carrington, Carter, Cary, Catlett, Chamberlayne, Christian, Clopton, Claiborne, Clayton, Clarke, Cocke, Coleman, Coles, Colston, Cooper, Conway, Corbin, Custis, Crawford.

Dabney, Daniel, Davenport, Davis, Dandridge, Digges, Dulany.

Edmunds, Edwards, Eggleston, Eldridge, Ellis, Embry, Eppes, Everard, Eyre.

Fairfax, Farley, Faulcon, Field, Fitzgerald, Fitzhugh, Fleming, Fry.

Gay, Gibbon, Gilmer, Goode, Goodwyn, Graves, Grayson, Green, Griffin, Grymes, Grammat, Greenway, Garnet, Garland, Gaines, Gholson.

Hackley, Hansford, Hardaway, Harmer, Harrison, Harvie, Herbert, Hill, Holliday, Holmes, Hooe, Howard, Hubard, Hairston, Heath, Heth, Hicks, Hopkins, Hawkins, Hodges, Henderson, Haynes.

Innes, Irby.

Jefferson, Jennings, Johnson, Jones, Joynes.

Kennon, King.

Lanier, Lee, Lewis, Lightfoot, Littlepage, Littleton, Lomax, Ludwell, Lyons, Leftwich.

Mallory, Martin, Marshall, Marye, Mason, Massie, Matthews, Mayo, Meade, Mercer, Minor, Meredith, Meriwether, Michie, Minge, McCarty, Moore, Moseley, Munford, Morris, Morton, Mosby.

Nash, Nelson, Newton, Nichols, Nivison, Norvell, Noland.

Page, Parke, Parker, Peachey, Pegram, Pendleton, Penn, Peter, Peyton, Phillips, Pierce, Pleasant, Pollard, Pope, Powell, Poythress, Prentice, Price, Prosser, Posey.

Randolph, Reade, Riddick, Roane, Robinson, Rose, Ruffin, Russell, Royall.

Savage, Saunders, Scarburgh, Selden, Shepherd, Short, Skelton, Skepwith, Slaughter, Spottswood, Stanard, Stevenson, Stith, Stokes, Steptoe, Strother, Swann, Syme, Spencer,

Tabb, Talbot, Taliafero, Tayloe, Taylor, Tazewell, Terry, Thornton, Todd, Travis, Trent, Tucker, Tyler.

Upshur, Upshaw: Venable, Vaughn.

Waller, Walker, Walton, Wade, Ward, Waryng, Washington, Watkins, Watson, West, Wickham, Webb, Whiting, Westwood, Wilkins, Wilcox, Willis, Winston, Williams,Withers, Wood, Woodson, Wise, Wormley, Wyatt, Wythe.

Yates, Yelverton.

Most of the names in this list also occur in Savage's Dictionary of the Settlers of New England; two thirds of them are to be found in both places. The proof is as ample in the one case as the other. If the Virginians were gentlemen on account of their names, so were the Yankees.

Again, I give the following list of Delegates in 1776, comprising the most influential persons, but I do not find it an epitome of the English Peerage:

VIRGINIA CONVENTION, 1776.

Acrill, Adams, Aylett, Barrister, Berkeley, Bird, Blair, Bland, Booker, Bowyer, Brook, Bullitt, Burwell, Cabell, Campbell, Carrington, Cary, Clapham, Clayton, Cocke, Cowper, Cralle, Curle, Dandridge, Diggs, Drew, Edmundson, Farmer, Field, Fitzhugh, Fleming, Fulton, Garland, Gee, Gilmer, Goode, Gordon, Gray, Harrison, Harvie, Harwood, Henry, Hite, Hold, Jefferson, Johnson, Jones, Kenner, King, Lankford, Lee, Lewis, Lockhart, Lynch, Lyne, Maclin, MacDowell, McCarty, Madison, Mason, Mayo, Mercer, Meriwether, Montague, Moore, Muse, Nelson, Newton, Nicholas, Norvell, Page, Patterson, Pendleton, Penn, Peyton, Pickett, Poythress, Randolph, Reddick, Reed, Robinson, Russell, Rutherford, Savage, Scott, Selden, Simms, Simpson, Smith, Speed, Starko, Strother, Syme, Tabb, Talbot, Taylor, Tazewell, Terry, Thornton, Thoroughgood, Tipton, Travis, Washington, Watkins, Watts, West, Whiting, Wilkins, Williams, Winn, Wood, Woodson, Wythe, Zane.

NEW ENGLAND.

When we commence an examination of the ancestry of the settlers of New England, we find ourselves at once on sure ground. No other community possesses the same facilities for investigation. Our records are very full, they are open to inspection at all times, and a great number of them have been printed. We have the only Genealogical Society in the country, perhaps in the world, and in Savage's

"Dictionary of the Early Settlers of New England," we have a collection of genealogical information, such as no other community possesses of its ancestry. I will first give the statements, on the subject of the nationality of our ancestors, as presented by HUTCHINSON, SAVAGE, and PALFREY, and the earlier authorities, RANDOLPH and BRADSTREET.

In 1776. The Lords of the Privy Council sent to New England divers inquiries, as to the present state of the colony. Edmund Randolph's report, printed in Hutchinson's Collection of Papers, pp. 477—505, contains the following items:

P. 484 "The inhabitants within this government, including Hampshire and Maine, are computed to be upward of 150,000 souls. The chief professions are merchants, who are principally seated at Boston, Salem, Charlestown, and Portsmouth, and wealthy shop-keepers or retailers, who dwell in most towns of the colony, and get good estates. There are rich men of all callings and professions, and all mechanical arts and occupations thrive well.

The farmers are numerous and wealthy, live in good houses, are given to hospitality, and make good advantage by their corn, cattle, poultry, butter, and cheese.

There are about 30 merchants that are esteemed worth from £10,000 to £20,000; most have considerable estates, and very great trades, and are an industrious and thriving people. *There are no servants but upon hired wages,* except some few, who serve four years for the charge of being transported thither by their masters, and not above 200 slaves in the colony, and those are brought from Guinea and Madagascar.

There are men able to bear arms, between 30 and 40-000, and in the town of Boston, is computed about 4,000."

P. 502. "As to the Colonies of New-Plymouth and Connecticut,....the number of inhabitants in both colonies, is computed to be 80,000 souls. There are no slaves, only hired servants. The chief professions are farmers, graziers, and fishermen. Very few merchants, they being supplied with all foreign commodities, from Boston. The number fit to bear arms, 20,000."

Gov. Bradstreet replies to the same questions (See Mass. Historical Society's Collections, 3d series, viii, p. 336.) "There have been very few English come to plant in this jurisdiction for seven years past and more, and few or no Scots, Irish, or Foreigners in the like space; they rather go

to Carolina or other places more commodious, and less in-
habited, for with us, all the lands near the sea coast are ap-
propriated and improved, and up into the country is more
difficult (especially for new comers) to plant and subdue, and
must be done by the settled inhabitants by degrees, as divers towns already have been.

There hath been no company of blacks or slaves brought
into the country since the beginning of this plantation, for
the space of fifty years, only one small vessel about two years
since, after twenty months' voyage to Madagascar, brought
hither betwixt forty and fifty negroes, most women and children, sold here for £10, 15, 20, apiece, which stood the merchants in near £40, one with another.

Now and then, two or three negroes are brought hither
from Barbadoes and others of his Majesty's plantations, and
sold here for about £20 apiece, so that there may be within
our government, 100 to 120, and it may be as many Scots
brought hither and sold for servants, in the time of the war
with Scotland, and most now married and living here, and
about half so many Irish, brought here at several times as servants."

Hutchinson writes (History of Massachusetts, 1st ed. i,
93) under date of 1640: "The importation of settlers now
ceased. The motive to transportation to America was over
by the change in the affairs of England. They say who then
professed to be able to give the best account, that in 298
ships, which were the whole number from the beginning of
the colony, there arrived 21,200 passengers, men, women,
and children, perhaps about 4,000 families. Since which
more persons have removed out of New England to other
parts of the world, than have come from other parts to it,
and the number of families may be supposed to be less
rather than more than the natural increase of four thousand.

Again in the preface he writes: "The Massachusetts
colony may be considered as the parent of all the other colonies of New England. There was no importation of planters from England, to any part of the continent northward
of Maryland, except to the Massachusetts, for more than
fifty years after the colony began. In the first two years
about twenty thousand souls had arrived in the Massachusetts. Since then it is supposed more have gone hence to
England, than have come thence hither. Massachusetts-Bay,
New Hampshire, Connecticut, and Rhode Island, at this day
(1764) probably contain 500,000 souls. A surprising increase of subjects of the British crown!"

Palfrey writes in the Introduction to his History of New England: "The founders of the commonwealth of which I write, were Englishmen. Their emigration to New England began in 1620. It was inconsiderable till 1630. At the end of ten years more, it almost ceased. A people, consisting at that time of not many more than twenty thousand persons, thenceforward multiplied on its own soil, in remarkable seclusion from other communities, for nearly a century and a half. Some slight emigration from it took place at an early day ; but they were soon discontinued ; and it was not till the last quarter of the eighteenth century, that those swarms began to depart, which have since occupied so large a portion of the territory of the United States."

During that long period, and for many years later, their identity was unimpaired. No race has ever been more homogeneous than this remained, down to the time of the generation now upon the stage. With a near approach to precision, it may be said that the millions of living persons, either born in New England, or tracing their origin to natives of that region, are descendants of the twenty-one thousand Englishmen, who came over before the early emigration from England ceased upon the meeting of the Long Parliament. Such exceptions to this statement, as belong to any time preceding that of the present generation, are of small account. In 1651, after the battles of Dunbar and Worcester, Cromwell sent some four or five hundred of his Scotch prisoners to Boston; but very little trace of this accession is left. The discontented strangers took no root. After the revocation of the Edict of Nantes in 1685, about one hundred and fifty families of French Huguenots came to Massachusetts, where, though their names have mostly died out, a considerable number of their posterity are yet to be found. A hundred and twenty Scotch-Irish families came over in 1719, and settled in Londonderry, in New Hampshire and elsewhere. Great numbers of foreigners—especially of Irish, and, next to them, of Germans—are now to be reckoned in a census of New England; but it is chiefly within the last thirty years that they have come, and they remain for the most part unamalgamated with the population of English descent.

Thus the people of New England are a singularly un- . mixed race. There is probably not a county in England, occupied by a population of purer English blood than theirs. It is a race still more specially to be characterized as representing a peculiar type of the Englishmen of the seventeenth century. A large majority of the early planters were Puritans. Some of the small English settlements in the eastern part of the country were composed of other elements. But, from the early time when these were absorbed by Massachusetts, their anti-Puritan peculiarities began to disappear, and a substantial conformity to the Puritan standard, became universal.

Sequestered from foreign influences, the people thus constituted, was forming a distinct character by its own discipline, and was engaged at work within itself, on its own problems, through a century and a half. Down to the eve of the war which began in 1775, New England had little knowledge of the communities which took part with her in that conflict. Till the time of the Boston Port Bill, eighty-four years ago, Massachusetts and Virginia, the two principal English colonies, had with each other scarcely more relations of acquaintance, business, mutual influence, or common action, than either of them had with Jamaica or Quebec.

This people, so isolated in its pupilage, has now diffused itself. I am to tell the early story of a vast tribe of men, numbering at the present time, it is likely, some seven or eight millions. Exactness in such an estimate is not attainable; but it would probably be coming somewhere near the truth to divide the present white population of the United States into three equal parts; one, belonging to the New England stock; one, the posterity of English who settled in the other Atlantic colonies; and another, consisting of the aggregate of Irish, Scotch, French, Dutch, German, Swedish, Spanish, and other immigrants, and their descendants. According to the United States' Census of 1850, the six New England States had in that year 2,705,095 inhabitants, of which number 305,444 were of foreign birth. It would, I suppose, be making a liberal allowance to refer the round number of half a million of the present inhabitants of those States, to the modern immigrations from abroad. On the other hand, more than seven hundred and fifty thousand natives of New England,—often persons not inconsiderable in respect to activity, property or influence—are supposed to be now living in other parts of the Union. The New England race has contributed largely to the population of the great State of New York, and makes a majority in some of the new States further west. Considerable numbers of them are dispersed in distant parts of the world, where commerce or other business invites enterprise, though they do not often establish themselves for life in foreign countries. I presume there is one third of the people of these United States—wherever now residing—of whom no individual could peruse this volume, without reading the history of his own progenitors."

SAVAGE writes "That New-England was first occupied by a civilized people, in so short a period before the great civil war broke out in our mother country, though half a century and more after its elementary principles began to ferment, especially in Parliament, and almost in every parish in the Kingdom, was a very fortunate event, if it may not be thought a providential arrangement for the happiness of mankind. Even if our views be restricted to the lineal origin of those people here, when the long protracted impolicy of Great Britain, drove our fathers into open hostility, and forced them to become a nation in 1776, in that century and a half from its colonization, a purer Anglo Saxon race would be seen on this side of the ocean than on the other. Within forty years a vast influx of Irish, with not a few thousand Scotch and Germans, has spread over this new country, but certainly more than four-fifths of our people * still count their progenitors among the ante-revolutionary colonists.

From long and careful research, I have judged the proportion of the whole number living here in 1775, that deduce their origin from the Kingdom of England, i. e. the Southern part of Great Britain, excluding also the principality of Wales, to exceed ninety-eight in a hundred. Every county from Northumberland to Cornwall, Kent to Cumberland, sent its contribution of emigrants, and the sparse population of the narrow shire of Rutland had more than one offshoot in New England. But, during that interval, great was the diversity of circumstances between the old and new country, so far as the increase of their number by incoming of strangers was affected. In 1660, the restoration of Charles II — in 1685, the expulsion of the two hundred thousand Protestants from France, the desired invasion of William and Mary, in 1688, and the settlement of the House of Hanover, in 1714, each brought from the continent an infusion upon the original stock, the aggregate of which may not have been less than five or six per cent. of that into which it was ingrafted.

Yet hardly more than three in a thousand, for instance of Scottish ancestry, almost wholly the migration of the heroic defenders of Londonderry, that came as one hundred and twenty families in 1718 and 19, could be found in 1775, among dwellers on our soil; a smaller number still of the glorious Huguenot exiles above thirty years longer had been resident here, and may have been happy enough by natural increase (though I doubt it) to equal the latter band. If these be also counted three in a thousand, much fewer, though earler still, must be the Dutch that crept in from New York,

* Mr. Savage must be understood as speaking of New England.

chiefly to Connecticut, so that none can believe they reach two in a thousand; while something less must be the ratio of Irish. Germany, Italy, Sweden, Spain, Africa, and all the rest of the world, together, did not outnumber the Scotch or the French singly. A more homogeneous stock cannot be seen I think, in any so extensive a region, at any time since that when the ark of Noah discharged its passengers on Mount Ararat, except in the few centuries elapsing before the confusion of Babel.

What honorable ancestry the body of New England population may assert, has often been proclaimed in glowing language; but the words of William Stoughton, in his Election sermon, 1688, express the sentiment with no less happiness than brevity; 'GOD SIFTED A WHOLE NATION THAT HE MIGHT SEND CHOICE GRAIN INTO THE WILDERNESS'."

It seems almost superfluous to add any corroboration of these opinions ; yet the case may be strengthened by a detail of our authorities. Mr. SAVAGE's Dictionary, from the preface of which the previous paragraphs are cited, consists of four volumes embracing over twenty-five hundred, closely printed, octavo pages. He attempts to give the first three generations of those who settled in New England before 1692. However imperfect the book may be in the record of the children, he has unquestionably obtained the names of nineteen-twentieths of those who settled here previous to 1640, the date, when, as Hutchinson says, the immigration ceased, and these names confirm entirely his assertion, that the settlers were English. Of the 4000 heads of families, one third at least had taken the freeman's oath by that time, and their names are printed in the Massachusetts Records. Massachusetts, Plymouth, Rhode Island and Connecticut, have all issued volumes containing the early records of the respective colonies. Nearly all the older towns have their histories carefully prepared and printed. Of those not yet published, I believe hardly one can be named whose records have not been examined in aid of Mr. Savage, or for the use of our numerous genealogists. Our county registries of deeds, the records of births, marriages, and deaths, preserved in every town, and the registries of the different parishes, are all very complete, are open to inspection freely and gratuitously, and have been consulted by hundreds of our writers. We have a Genealogical Society, which has published seventeen annual volumes, averaging nearly four hundred pages each, devoted to the history of New England families. Genealogy has been a favorite study here, and, as Sir Bernard Burke writes, "for ten or twelve years before the civil conflict broke out, Massachusetts was more genealogical than Yorkshire, and Boston sustained what London never did, a magazine devoted exclusively to genealogy."

When I prepared a "Handbook of American Genealogy," in 1862, the list comprised 222 genealogies, 16 tabular pedigrees, and 59 town histories and collections, and of the genealogies, not half a dozen were of other than New England families. It is almost certain that there are extant more printed pages of genealogical information relative to the eight generations of families here, than there are relative to the history of English families since the Conquest.

Is it too much to claim, therefore, that we are dealing with facts and not conjectures, when we say that whatever was the case in other colonies, New England was and is thoroughly English and homogeneous?

In pursuance of the plan adopted, having shown the nationality of the colonists of New England, it is necessary to speak of their social position prior to their emigration from England. Having demonstrated that our ancestors were not convicts, nor the outcasts of society swept from the wretched dens of the great cities by a disdainful charity, anxious only to be rid of them, we might well pause, content to say that they were at least equal to the ancestors of that portion of the English people of the present day, which includes the respectable classes.

As however a false impression has been given by the use of the terms Cavalier and Roundhead, let us pursue the investigation a little farther. MACAULAY has sketched the origin of these parties, and familiar as his descriptions may be, we may here repeat them. He says "when, in October, 1641, the Parliament reässembled, after a short recess, two hostile parties, essentially the same with those, which, under different names, have ever since contended, and are still contending, for the direction of public affairs, appeared confronting each other. During some years they were designated as Cavaliers and Roundheads. They were subsequently called Tories and Whigs, nor does it seem that these appellations are likely soon to become obsolete."

"When the rival parties first appeared in a distinct form they seemed to be not unequally matched. On the side of the government was a large majority of the nobles and of those opulent and well-descended gentlemen to whom nothing was wanting of nobility but the name. These, with the dependents whose support they could command, were no small power in the state. On the same side were the great body of the clergy, both the universities and all those laymen who were strongly attached to episcopal government, and to the Anglican ritual. These respectable classes found themselves in the company of some allies much less decorous than themselves. The Puritan austerity drove to the kings' faction, all who made pleasure their business, who affected gallantry, splendor of dress, or taste in the lighter arts. With these went all who live by amusing the leisure of others, from the painter and comic poet, down to the rope-dancer and Merry Andrew, for these artists well knew they might thrive under a superb and luxurious despotism, but must starve under the rigid rule of the precisians."

"The main strength of the Opposition lay among the small freeholders in the country, and among the merchant and shop-keepers of the towns. But these were headed by a formidable minority of the aristocracy; a minority which included the rich and powerful Earls of Northumberland, Bedford, Warwick, Stamford, and Essex, and several other lords of great wealth and influence. In the same ranks were found the whole body of Protestant Non-conformists, and most of those members of the Established Church, who still adhered to the Calvinistic opinions, which, forty years before, had been generally held by the prelates and clergy. The municipal corporations took, with few exceptions, the same side. In the House of Commons, the Opposition preponderated, but not very decidedly."

We see by this statement, that the Cavaliers of Charles' time were not a class distinct from the Roundheads. Even the absurd distinction which Southern writers attempt to make, is untenable. The Cavaliers were no better gentlemen than their opponents ; and the preponderance in the proportion was probably in favor of the Puritans.

A slight digression may render plainer a matter which has been obscured by the falsehoods of Southern writers and their English allies. A gentleman, in English Heraldry, taking the largest definition, is a man whose ancestors at a certain time used coats-of-arms, and had a certain rank. This gentility of birth being inheritable may descend to a person of any rank ; the proof of his pedigree being all sufficient. Of late years, the rule has fallen into neglect, and probably not one quarter of the Englishmen who style themselves gentlemen, and use armorial bearings, could establish their rights. In common usage, this distinction being forgotten, we term a man a gentleman by birth whose ancestors have possessed wealth and social position for two or three generations. Now, accepting this definition, it is easily to be proved that a greater number, perhaps a greater proportion, of our New England settlers were of this rank than in the whole of the colonies embraced in the Confederate States. The whole point is one of enumeration and figures, and does not properly belong to this essay. Should the assertion be questioned, the facts can easily be produced, and names given. More than this, in the heraldric sense, New England possesses a much larger proportion of gentle blood than the entire South. No one supposes that very many representatives of old English families abandoned their homes and came to New England, Virginia, or the Carolinas. But the great middle class of that day did send forth a great number from its ranks to New England, even as the workhouses and gaols sent their swarms to people Virginia and the other Southern colonies.

The old county families must have contributed largely to the very class from which our ancestors here were supplied. The men who lost their lands by war, by subdivision or misfortune, the whole category of younger sons, all contributed to the class of merchants and tradespeople, which rose to such importance during the reigns of Elizabeth and James. Whoever considers the present condition of the laboring population of England, and their probable position two centuries ago, will feel convinced that it was not there, that we should find men with the means, intelligence, and devotion, which the early emigrants possessed.

It is impossible to discuss here the question of the percentage of gentle blood in New England. Such discussions belong to genealogists, and are too personal and trivial to be suffered to draw us from the main point. We are content with our ancestors, so far as we can trace their history in this country; it is only in reply to the falsehoods of our opponents, that we need retort.

If we leave the dry details, which I have presented simply as indications of the method in which this question can be discussed, and regard the problem in a more general view, it is surprising to see how theory and fact agree. The United States are essentially English to-day, despite the millions of foreigners which have been absorbed into its population. The tendency of its citizens has been toward a democracy, and yet not toward anarchy and lawlessness. The throes of a gigantic revolution have not sufficed to outweigh the instinctive love of law and order, peculiar to the English race.

When we enquire what controlling influence has impressed this form upon the national character, the enemies of the predominant party instinctively show that it is New England. Not the comparatively limited New England of 1863, but the New England stock and influence, which has invigorated nearly every State of the Union. In their ignorance of the past, these revilers of New England have been blindly attacking a greater fact than they were aware of. Not only is nearly a third part of our native-born population the offspring of the New England of the Revolution, but long before that time the intermixture had commenced. Whitehead's "New Jersey" (p. 159) quotes Governor Burnet's letter, written in 1729:

"The people of New Jersey (being generally of New

England extraction, and therefore enthusiasts) would consider the number of planters, etc., as a repetition of the same sin as David committed in numbering the people."

The History of Dorchester, Massachusetts, quotes a letter from the Secretary of Georgia, in 1755, in relation to a colony from that town, in which he says:

"I really look upon these people moving here to be one of the most favorable circumstances that could befall the colony."

It is added:

"This settlement has furnished Georgia with two governors, two of its most distinguished judges, the theological seminary of South Carolina and Georgia with an able professor, the Methodist Episcopal Church with an influential and pious bishop, the Presbyterian and Baptist Churches of that State with many of their ablest and most useful ministers; and six of her sons have been called away to professional chairs in collegiate institutions."

The first attempt at colonizing the Mississippi delta, was made by the Lymans, Dwights, and their associates from Connecticut. New York received a constant accession from New England long before 1775.

Here, then, history and theory both agree. New England, colonized by Englishmen, homogeneous in a remarkable degree, has been the only thoroughly pure nationality within our territories. The few stray Englishmen of education in the Southern colonies, the much greater number of convicts, the increasing immigration of French, Irish, Scotch, and German settlers, have not only failed to overwhelm this compact and thoroughly alive minority, but have been formed and moulded into shape by it. In protesting against New England, the Vallandighams and Coxes are only proving the nullity of "expunging resolutions." "Can they make that not to be which has been?" Until they can recall the past, annihilate the past inhabitants of these States, and from stones raise up some other progenitors for the present generation, they cannot destroy the influence of New England.

And yet we are called upon to believe that the race which has thus done the greatest work of the past two centuries, was the random aggregation of opposite and mongrel races, the offspring of ignorance, poverty, and crime. We are to believe that while the pure blood of English gentlemen in Virginia, has produced not only the gentlemanly vices of pride, treachery, and falsehood in the leaders, but the ignoble faults of crime and debasement in the "poor trash," that some occult influence of climate has advanced an entire community at the North far above the position of its progenitors—that while the gentle Cavalier has been overcome by the seductive charms of luxury and repose, the ignoble Puritan has thrown off his degrading antecedents, and has obtained the control of the allied races. The servant has become the master, the scum of all nations has overpowered the choicest offspring of that race which Macaulay terms "the hereditary rulers of mankind."

These conclusions, so eminently logical and convincing. we must believe, or we must doubt the pure blood of the aristocracy of the Slave States.

Is it not more reasonable to believe, as facts daily prove. that New England was colonized from the hardiest and best portion of the English stock ? That our ancestors, accepting the state of English society as a fact, neither invited nor repelled the accession of the gentry. That many of that class did join in the enterprise, and that, where they were worthy, they received the slight preference which is accorded to personal advantages of any sort. That the bulk of the colonists were separated from this class by slight barriers, that many of them were excluded only by a want of the necessary property to maintain the position, and that on this new territory, these distinctions were speedily forgotton— not because the higher class deteriorated, but because the lower, having but a slight advance to make, soon stood on an actual equality with them.

If the sympathy of England were now as desirable and as strongly expected as it was two years ago, I might urge the matter further. As it is, it seems sufficient to overthrow the claims of Southerners, based upon false pretenses, and supported only by unblushing effrontery, and to refute the slanders which have been thrown upon an entire section of the loyal States.